*A book
is a present you can open
again and again.*

THIS BOOK BELONGS TO

_____

FROM

_____

Anytime Rhymes

WRIGGLES &
GIGGLES

Illustrated by Blanche L. Sims

TREASURE TREE ™

World Book, Inc.
a Scott Fetzer company
Chicago London Sydney Toronto

Copyright © 1992
World Book, Inc.
525 West Monroe Street
Chicago, Illinois 60661

Printed in the United States of America
ISBN 0-7166-1610-6
Library of Congress Catalog Card No. 91-65492

5 6 7 8 9 10 11 12 13 14 15 99 98 97 96 95 94

Cover design by Rosa Cabrera
Book design by Valerie Nelson-Metlay

Fuzzy Wuzzy was a bear,
Fuzzy Wuzzy had no hair.
Fuzzy Wuzzy wasn't fuzzy,
Was he?

Algy met a bear,
A bear met Algy.
The bear was bulgy,
The bulge was Algy.

My shoes are new and squeaky shoes,
They're very shiny, creaky shoes.
I wish I had my leaky shoes
That mother threw away.

I liked my old brown leaky shoes
Much better than these creaky shoes—
These shiny, creaky, squeaky shoes
I've got to wear today.

As I was going out one day
My head fell off and rolled away.
But when I saw that it was gone,
I picked it up and put it on.

And when I got into the street
A fellow cried: "Look at your feet!"
I looked at them and sadly said:
"I've left them both asleep in bed!"

The lion walks on padded paws,
The squirrel leaps from limb to limb,
While flies can crawl straight up a wall,
And seals can dive and swim.
The worm, it wiggles all around,
The monkey swings by its tail,
And birds may hop upon the ground
Or spread their wings and sail.
But boys and girls have much more fun;
They leap and dance
And walk
And *run.*

Five tiny green peas, lying in a row
Inside a small green pod, one day began to grow.
They grew and they grew and they didn't stop
Until one day their pod went POP!

A peanut sat on a railroad track.
His heart was all aflutter.
The five-fifteen came rushing by—
Toot! Toot! Peanut butter!

I always eat my peas with honey,
I've done it all my life.
It makes them taste kind of funny,
But it keeps them on the knife.

There were three ghostesses
Sitting on postesses
Eating buttered toastesses
And greasing their fistesses
Right up to their wristesses.
Weren't they beastesses
To make such feastesses!

"Bubble," said the kettle,
"Bubble," said the pot.
"Bubble, bubble, bubble,
We are getting very hot!"

Shall I take you off the fire?
"No, you need not trouble.
This is just the way we talk—
Bubble, bubble, bubble!"

Betty Botter bought some butter,
"But," she said, "the butter's bitter.
If I put it in my batter,
It will make my batter bitter.
But a bit of better butter,
That would make my batter better."
So she bought a bit of butter
Better than her bitter butter,
And she put it in her batter
And the batter was not bitter.
So 'twas better Betty Botter
Bought a bit of better butter.

I raised a great hullabaloo
When I found a large mouse in my stew.
   Said the waiter, "Don't shout
   And wave it about,
Or the rest will be wanting one too!"

You've no need to light a night light
On a light night like tonight,
For a night light's light's a slight light,
And tonight's a night that's light.

When a night's light, like tonight's light,
It is really not quite right
To light night lights with their slight-lights
On a light night like tonight.

There was a young lady of Crete,
Who was so exceedingly neat,
  When she got out of bed
  She stood on her head,
To make sure of not soiling her feet.

Saw a flea kick a tree,
Fooba wooba fooba wooba,
Saw a flea kick a tree,
Fooba wooba John.
Saw a flea kick a tree in the middle of the sea,
Fooba wooba, fooba wooba,
Fooba wooba John.

Saw a crow flying low,
Fooba wooba fooba wooba,
Saw a crow flying low,
Fooba wooba John.
Saw a crow flying low several miles beneath the snow,
Fooba wooba, fooba wooba,
Fooba wooba John.

Saw a bug give a shrug,
Fooba wooba fooba wooba,
Saw a bug give a shrug,
Fooba wooba John.
Saw a bug give a shrug in the middle of the rug,
Fooba wooba, fooba wooba,
Fooba wooba John.

Saw a whale chase a snail,
Fooba wooba fooba wooba,
Saw a whale chase a snail,
Fooba wooba John.
Saw a whale chase a snail all around a water pail,
Fooba wooba, fooba wooba,
Fooba wooba John.

Saw two geese making cheese,
Fooba wooba fooba wooba,
Saw two geese making cheese,
Fooba wooba John.
Saw two geese making cheese one would hold and the other would squeeze.
Fooba wooba, fooba wooba,
Fooba wooba John.

Saw a mule teaching school,
Fooba wooba fooba wooba,
Saw a mule teaching school,
Fooba wooba John.
Saw a mule teaching school to some bullfrogs in the pool,
Fooba wooba, fooba wooba,
Fooba wooba John.

Saw a bee off to sea,
Fooba wooba fooba wooba,
Saw a bee off to sea,
Fooba wooba John.
Saw a bee off to sea with his fiddle across his knee,
Fooba wooba, fooba wooba,
Fooba wooba John.

Saw a hare chase a deer,
Fooba wooba fooba wooba,
Saw a hare chase a deer,
Fooba wooba John.
Saw a hare chase a deer ran it all of seven year,
Fooba wooba, fooba wooba,
Fooba wooba John.

Saw a bear scratch his ear,
Fooba wooba fooba wooba,
Saw a bear scratch his ear,
Fooba wooba John.
Saw a bear scratch his ear wonderin' what we're doing here,
Fooba wooba, fooba wooba,
Fooba wooba John.

Once upon a time, in a little wee house,
   Lived a funny old man and his wife;
And he said something funny to make her laugh,
   Every day of his life.

One day he said such a funny thing,
   That she shook and screamed with laughter;
But the poor old soul, she couldn't leave off
   For at least three whole days after.

So laughing with all her might and main,
   Three days and nights she sat;
And at the end she didn't know a bit
   What she'd been laughing at.

Somebody loves you deep and true.
If I weren't so bashful, I'd tell you who.

I love you, I love you,
I love you divine.
Please give me your bubble gum,
You're sitting on mine!

The elephant carries a great big trunk;
He never packs it with clothes;
It has no lock and it has no key,
But he takes it wherever he goes.

Way down South, where bananas grow,
A grasshopper stepped on an elephant's toe.
The elephant cried with tears in his eyes,
"Why don't you pick on someone your own size?"

Whisky, frisky
Hippity hop,
Up he goes
To the treetop!

Whirly, twirly,
Round and round,
Down he scampers
To the ground.

Furly, curly,
What a tail!
Tall as a feather,
Broad as a sail!

Where's his supper?
In the shell,
Snappity, crackity,
Out it fell!

Three young rats with black felt hats,
Three young ducks with white straw flats,
Three young dogs with curling tails,
Three young cats with demiveils,
Went out to walk with two young pigs
In satin vests and sorrel wigs,
But suddenly it changed to rain,
And so they all went home again.

I had a little pig,
I fed him in a trough,
He got so fat
His tail dropped off.
So I got me a nail,
And I made my little pig
A brand new tail.

Curious fly,
Vinegar jug,
Slippery edge,
Pickled bug.

A fly and a flea in a flue
Were imprisoned, so what could they do?
    Said the fly, "Let us flee!"
    "Let us fly!" said the flea,
And they flew through a flaw in the flue.

My father owns the butcher shop,
My mother cuts the meat,
And I'm the little hot dog
That runs around the street.

There was a little dog and he had a little tail,
And he used to wag, wag, wag it!
But when he was sad because he'd been bad,
On the ground he would drag, drag, drag it!

finest
Hot
Dogs

The joke you told just isn't funny one bit.
It's pointless and dull, wholly lacking in wit.
It's so old and stale, it's beginning to smell!
Besides, it's the one I was going to tell.

One day a boy went walking
And went into a store;
He bought a pound of sausages
And laid them on the floor.

The boy began to whistle
A merry little tune—
And all the little sausages
Danced around the room!

"**G**o, my son, and shut the shutter."
This I heard a mother utter.
"Shutter's shut," the boy did mutter.
"I can't shut 'er any shutter."

Doctor Bell fell down the well
And broke his collarbone.
Doctors should attend the sick
And leave the well alone.

There's music in a hammer.
There's music in a nail.
There's music in a pussycat
When you step upon her tail.

One, two, three, four, five!
"Once I caught a fish alive!"
Six, seven, eight, nine, ten!
"Then I let it go again."
"Why did you let it go?"
"Because it bit my finger so."
"Which finger did it bite?"
"This finger on my right!"

Did you ever go fishing on a bright sunny day—
Sit on a fence and have the fence give way?
Slide off the fence and rip your pants,
And see the little fishes do the hootchy-kootchy dance?

A sea serpent saw a big tanker,
Bit a hole in her side, and then sank her.
  It swallowed the crew
  In a minute or two—
And then picked its teeth with the anchor.

Behold the wonders of the mighty deep,
Where crabs and lobsters learn to creep,
And little fishes learn to swim,
And clumsy sailors tumble in.

Whether the weather be fine,
Or whether the weather be not,
Whether the weather be cold,
Or whether the weather be hot,
We'll weather the weather
Whatever the weather,
Whether we like it or not!

Spring is showery, flowery, bowery.
Summer: hoppy, croppy, poppy.
Autumn: wheezy, sneezy, freezy.
Winter: slippy, drippy, nippy.

I often sit and wish that I
Could be a kite up in the sky,
And ride upon the breeze and go
Whichever way I chanced to blow.

I'm glad the sky is painted blue,
And the earth is painted green,
With such a lot of nice fresh air
All sandwiched in between.

Once there was a snowman
  Stood outside the door
Thought he'd like to come inside
  And run around the floor;
Thought he'd like to warm himself
  By the firelight red;
Thought he'd like to climb up
  On that big white bed.
So he called the North Wind, "Help me now, I pray.
  I'm completely frozen, standing here all day."
So the North Wind came along and blew him in the door,
  And now there's nothing left of him
But a puddle on the floor!

I come to work as well as play;
   I'll tell you what I do;
I whistle all the live-long day,
   "Woo-oo-oo! Woo-oo!"

I toss the branches up and down
   And shake them to and fro,
I whirl the leaves in flocks of brown,
   And send them high and low.

I strew the twigs upon the ground,
   The frozen earth I sweep;
I blow the children round and round
   And wake the flowers from sleep.

Rain on the green grass,
   And rain on the tree,
And rain on the housetop,
   But not on me!

Here's to July,
Here's to July,
For the bird,
And the bee,
And the butterfly;
For the flowers
That blossom
For feasting the eye;
For skates, balls,
And jump ropes,
For swings that go high;
For rocketry
Fireworks that
Blaze in the sky,
Oh, here's to July!

In August, when the days are hot,
I like to find a shady spot,
And hardly move a single bit—
And sit—
    And sit—
        And sit!

The leaves had a wonderful frolic,
   They danced to the wind's loud song,
They whirled, and they floated, and scampered,
   They circled and flew along.

The moon saw the little leaves dancing,
   Each looked like a small brown bird.
The man in the moon smiled and listened,
   And this is the song he heard.

The North wind is calling, is calling,
   And we must whirl round and round,
And when our dancing is ended
   We'll make a warm quilt for the ground.

In jumping and tumbling
   We spend the whole day,
Till night by arriving
   Has finished our play.

What then? One and all,
   There's no more to be said,
As we tumbled all day,
   So we tumble to bed.

To Parents

Children delight in hearing and reading poems. *Wriggles & Giggles*
is filled with funny poems that will amuse your child and provide
a bridge into learning some important concepts. Here are a few easy
and natural ways your child can express feelings and
understandings about the poems. You know your child and
can best judge which ideas he or she will enjoy most.

This book is full of animals. While you are sharing a poem, ask your child how the animals in the poem are similar to or different from real animals. Then encourage your child to look through books, magazines, or catalogs for pictures of the animals you have talked about. You might want to make an animal scrapbook. You or your child can copy poems from this book to put in your book.

Poems can be about things that are both real and make-believe. After reading a poem, ask your child to help you decide which things could really happen and which could not. For example, do birds really make homes in trees? Do elephants really talk?

Many children enjoy playing rhyming games. As you and your child share poems, read up to a word that rhymes with another word in the poem. Then pause. Encourage your child to supply a rhyming word. Your child's response may be the word in the poem, or one that makes an interesting new version.

You and your child may have fun making up new verses to favorite poems, or making up original poems. An original poem can be created by changing a word or two in each line of a poem. If you want to keep the poems that your child makes up, you can tape-record them or write them down as your child speaks. Your child may even want to write poems without your help. Ask your child to draw you a picture to go with the poem. Encourage your child to share the poem with other members of your family.

To add variety to rereadings, pick poems to act out. For example, act out a poem for your child, then have him or her find the poem in the book. Take turns so that everyone has a chance to be an actor or a guesser.